KU-739-727

HEADStart

WILD
ANIMALS

KINGSTON UPON THAMES
PUBLIC LIBRARIES

06597 440

ALL	CLASS
TD	J59a
CAT	REF
P£3·95	2/02

First published in Great Britain by
CAXTON EDITIONS
an imprint of
The Caxton Book Company,
16 Connaught Street,
Marble Arch, London, W2 2AF.

Copyright © 1998 CAXTON EDITIONS

All rights reserved. No part of this publication may be reproduced, stored in a retrieval
system, or transmitted, in any form, or by any means, without the prior written permission
of the copyright holder.

ISBN 1 84067 058 4

A copy of the CIP data for this book is available from the British Library upon request.

With grateful thanks to Morse Modaberi who designed this book.

Created and produced for Caxton Editions by
FLAME TREE PUBLISHING,
a part of The Foundry Creative Media Company Ltd,
Crabtree Hall, Crabtree Lane,
Fulham, London, SW6 6TY.

Printed in Singapore by Star Standard Industries Pte. Ltd.

HEADstart

WILD ANIMALS

The world's best loved creatures, featured in glorious colour

CAMILLA DE LA BÉDOYÈRE

CAXTON EDITIONS

Contents

Introduction

Wild animals of the world live hard lives; they have to find food, homes and mates. They must be strong enough to fight disease, keep enemies away and protect their young. Many of them also have to fight with people for the land they need. Some animals, like tigers and pandas, may be losing these battles. Others, like foxes and bats, are more successful.

There are many types of wild animal – being different can help them to survive. The crocodile lives in rivers, the lion lives on grassland and the walrus lives in the freezing seas of the North. All these animals have changed over millions of years to suit the part of the world where they live.

People have been on this planet for a very short time but we have had a huge effect on the world and its creatures. Farming began 10,000 years ago and wild animals were tamed to provide ready forms of food. Cows, pigs, horses and sheep were once all wild animals. Since then people have spread across the world, farming the land, fishing the sea and taking what they wanted.

Now people have explored many parts of the world and we have learnt much more about it. We have discovered that the things we do can change the world and its creatures, perhaps forever. We understand that, wherever possible, animals should be allowed to live their lives in the wild, where they belong.

Tigers

The tiger belongs to the same family as lions, leopards, cheetahs and other big cats. It is the largest of all of these, and the rarest. Like all cats, tigers have sharp teeth and claws and hunt other animals to eat.

There are two main types of tiger; the Siberian and the Bengal and both of these live in Asia. They live in forests and can survive the cold winters and steaming, hot summers. The Siberian tiger is the largest of all big cats and is 3 metres long from head to tail. Most tigers are rust coloured with dark stripes but there is a type of Bengal tiger which has white fur with dark stripes.

Tigers live alone, roaming through their territory, or homeland, searching for prey. A tiger's territory is very large. Tigers eat meat; they attack deer, cattle and pigs but will even eat insects and frogs if they are hungry. They hunt in the evening when the light is low. A tiger's stripes help him to hide among the dense plants of the forest.

Tigers only come together to mate. The female has a litter of one to six cubs and she looks after them until they are two years old.

Tigers are very rare; one hundred years ago there were 50,000 tigers but now there are fewer than 5,000 tigers left in the wild. Most have been hunted for their skins and much of their land has been taken to grow crops.

Orang Utans

The name 'orang utan' means 'man of the forest' and it is a good name for these animals. With their long red hair and human-like faces orang utans look very much like people. They belong to the same group of animals as gorillas, chimps and humans.

Sadly, very few orang utans live in the wild now because their homes, the forests of Borneo and Sumatra, are being cut down to make way for humans' homes and farms. Many orang utans have also been killed by hunters.

Unlike gorillas, orang utans like to live in trees, where they spend most of the day eating leaves and fruit such as bananas and figs. Orang utans' bodies are perfect for swinging through trees: they have long arms and hands with fingers and thumbs for grabbing on to branches and they have short legs and no tail.

Groups of orang utans live together, eating during the day and sleeping at night in nests that rest on branches in the trees. They travel through the forests, searching for food. Babies cling tightly to their mother by gripping on to her fur as she swings from tree to tree. Orang utans are very clever animals and the young ones enjoy playing.

Males do not live in the groups; they travel through the forest alone and only join a group for mating. Adult males are much bigger than the females. They have a large air sac in their throats that they puff up to call loudly to other orang utans across the deep forest.

Kangaroos

Australia is home to some very unusual creatures – the marsupials. Like other mammals, they have fur and give birth to live babies who drink milk from their mothers.
But, unlike other mammals, the babies grow up in a pouch on their mother's belly. Koalas, wombats and kangaroos are all marsupials and are found in the wild only in Australia and nearby islands.

The largest marsupial is the red kangaroo which grows to 2 m in length. A baby red kangaroo is called a joey and it is only 2 cm long. A joey is born after growing for only five weeks inside its mother. It then crawls through her fur to the pouch where it continues to grow for another six months, feeding on its mother's milk. The joey can now begin to leave the pouch and explore the world outside, returning to its mother less frequently as it gets older.

Kangaroos live on grassland where they spend most of the day grazing. They move fairly slowly, but if attacked they can leap away using their powerful back legs. A long tail helps them to balance and change direction as they jump. A kangaroo can cover 8 metres with one bound, and jump a 3-metre high fence.

Kangaroos live in family groups called pods. Each pod contains one male, several females and their joeys. Dingos, Australian wild dogs, are their natural predators but adult kangaroos can defend themselves with a strong kick and sharp claws. Joeys are attacked by eagles and foxes. Kangaroos are also hunted by humans for their meat.

Giant Pandas

The forest-covered mountains of Western China are home to one of the world's rarest animals, the giant panda. Among the fine mists the panda wanders, munching on its favourite food – bamboo, a tall and slender plant that grows well in these forest areas.

Pandas have sharp claws and teeth but they rarely hunt or eat meat. Sometimes they catch rats which they enjoy but mostly they just eat bamboo. Unfortunately, this food does not have much goodness in it and an adult male needs 15 kg of bamboo a day to survive. Problems arise when humans cut down large areas of bamboo in order to build houses and farms.

Pandas prefer to live alone and only come together at mating time. A baby panda is called a cub and is very small: only 10 cm long. Cubs are completely white when born but when they are three weeks old they develop their black marks. Usually two babies are born but one dies soon afterwards. The mother looks after her cub with great care; cuddling it gently in her paws all day and all night. The cub takes milk from its mother and does not leave her side until it is 18 months old.

Although pandas can be fierce fighters they are usually slow and gentle animals. Their natural enemies are leopards and jackals.

There are only 1,500 giant pandas left in the wild and they may soon become extinct. Pandas are kept in zoos all over the world, but it is very unusual for these captive pandas to have cubs. This makes conservationists worry if this beautiful species of animal will be able to survive.

Walruses

Life in the freezing Arctic Circle is not easy, but some animals do survive in these harsh conditions. The mighty walrus is one of them. Unlike their cousins – seals and sea lions – walruses live only in the cold waters of the North Atlantic and Pacific Oceans.

Male walruses are bigger than the females; they may reach 3 metres in length and weigh up to 1.5 tonnes. Adults have huge ivory tusks that grow down from their mouths; these are really very large teeth and may be up to 1 metre long in males. These tusks are sometimes used for fighting but walruses are usually gentle creatures and mainly use their tusks to pull themselves up on to land.

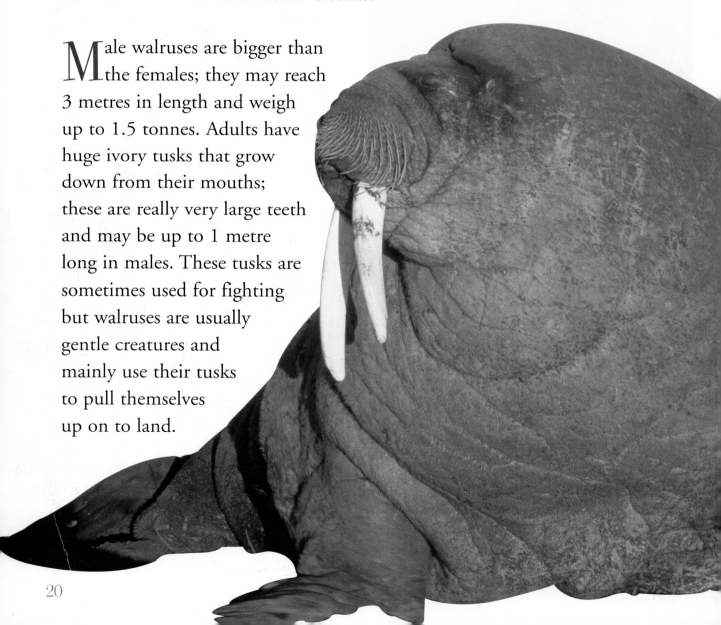

Walruses have thick, wrinkled and hairy skin. Underneath there is a thick layer of fat that keeps them warm in the coldest winter weather. They spend a lot of time underwater searching for food, mainly shellfish, using their sensitive whiskers. They are not very good swimmers and often hitch a ride on passing slabs of ice.

Although walruses spend much of their time in the water they have to give birth on land. The babies are called calves and are fed on their mothers' milk. Mothers guard their babies carefully and will fight to defend them. Until they learn how to swim the calves travel on their mothers' backs.

Walruses live in large groups, called herds, which may have several thousand members. Their natural predators are killer whales and people.

Foxes

Foxes are a type of wild dog and they are found all over Africa, America, Asia and Europe. They are very successful wild animals: foxes can adjust to live in many different places and eat a great variety of food.

Red foxes are the most common of all foxes. They have reddish brown fur, black feet and a white tip to their tails. With sharp hearing and a keen sense of smell they are good hunters, usually eating mice, rabbits and voles. If foxes can not find any meat they will eat berries, fruit or food taken from rubbish bins.

A female fox, a 'vixen', has one litter of four to five cubs every year. When the cubs are born they are blind, like puppies, and their parents take care of them in the den until they are old enough to explore outside. It is believed that once a male and female fox have mated they will stay together for life. This type of permanent pairing is unusual in the animal world.

Many of the woods and fields where foxes once lived have been dug up to make way for new houses and foxes have had to find different places to live. Unlike most wild animals foxes are adaptable; many now live in towns instead of the countryside. In towns they live in gardens or near railways and they can find plenty of food in rubbish bins. In the countryside foxes are not very popular as they sometimes kill small farm animals, like chickens and ducks.

Sloths

If someone is called 'slothful' it means they are lazy and the sloths of Central and South America are possibly the laziest animals alive.

Sloths live only in trees and they spend most of their lives upside-down, hanging from branches. Their claws hook on to branches without the sloths having to use any muscle strength to hold themselves up. This means they can hang for hours without getting tired. Sloths even sleep like this, with their heads tucked between their arms. They prefer to feed at night and sleep during the day.

Leaves and shoots are all the food sloths need; they do not spend much energy so they can eat food

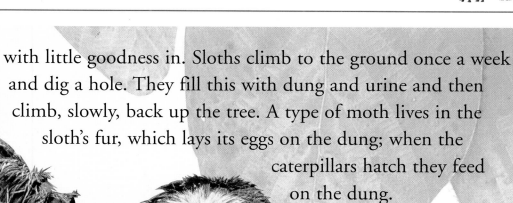

with little goodness in. Sloths climb to the ground once a week and dig a hole. They fill this with dung and urine and then climb, slowly, back up the tree. A type of moth lives in the sloth's fur, which lays its eggs on the dung; when the caterpillars hatch they feed on the dung.

Keeping very still is one way to hide from a predator and colouring yourself to fit in with the plants around you is another. A tiny green plant, called algae, grows in the fur of a sloth, turning it green. One of the sloth's natural enemies is the jaguar; even with its good eyes a jaguar may mistake a sloth for part of a tree.

Every spring female sloths have one baby. The baby hangs from the mother until it is old enough to take care of itself.

Wolves

The wolf, a cousin of our tame dogs, is a fierce hunter with sharp teeth and a fine sense of smell. People are often scared of wolves, but actually, they are shy and it is very rare for a wolf to attack a human.

Once there were many types of wolf living in North America, Europe and Asia but as people have used up more land, most of these have become extinct.

The biggest wolves live near the Arctic Circle, mainly in Canada. These animals are white or grey in colour, to blend in with the snowy landscape. They hunt large mammals like moose or caribou. Smaller wolves live in warmer countries and can be grey, brown or red. Because of their size they prey on smaller animals such as antelope or rabbits.

Wolves live in family packs, led by a female and male. These leaders are called the 'alpha pair' and are the only wolves in the pack to have young.

There are between four and seven cubs in a litter and they are born blind and deaf. Cubs are cared for by their mother, and by other females in the pack.

The alpha pair leads the hunt. Although wolves can hunt on their own they are more successful when they hunt together. It is important to communicate with each other to hunt well and wolves are good at this. They use body language; moving their ears, tails and lips to give a message. They also use barking and howling to communicate.

Crocodiles

Crocodiles are reptiles, like lizards, snakes and dinosaurs. They have scaly skin, lay their eggs on land and their bodies remain at the same temperature as the air or water around them.

Crocodiles live in warm parts of the world and are common in Africa and Central and South America. They live by lakes and rivers and spend most of the day resting in the water or sunbathing next to it.

With their powerful jaws and sharp teeth crocodiles are deadly hunters. They lie in wait for another animal to pass by, keeping still, with their bodies under water so that they are hidden and only their eyes and nostrils can be seen. A crocodile moves with great speed in order to catch its prey; he grabs an animal in his mouth then pulls it below the water surface and thrashes from side to side until it is dead.

When it is time to lay their eggs crocodiles build nests in sand or mud and leave the eggs to be warmed by the sun. Sometimes the mothers will stay near the nest to protect the eggs but, even with this care, many of the baby crocodiles will be caught and eaten. The babies are 30 cm long when they hatch and they live on land, eating insects and frogs until they are old enough to move in to the water.

Crocodiles have been hunted by humans for their skins for many years; as a result some species, in particular the American crocodile and the Nile crocodile, are in danger of dying out completely.

Grizzly Bears

Of all the wild bears the grizzlies are among the most dangerous. They live in North America, Canada and Alaska where people have invaded the bears' natural habitat by clearing the forests and building houses. Grizzlies may hunt for food on farms or they may go to people's homes if they can smell cooking or rubbish. If they are stopped from getting what they want, they may attack.

Many grizzly bears live in National Parks where they collect food the human visitors have left behind. They root through bins and have even been known to open locked cars to get at any titbits inside. Because bears have a very good sense of smell they are able to find food that is far away.

Grizzly bears eat grass, berries, nuts and meat. They enjoy fresh salmon and stand at a river's edge to catch the fish with their long, curled claws. These claws can also be used for digging small animals out of their burrows and ripping open beehives to get at the honey.

Grizzlies like to live alone and mark their homeland by snapping or chewing branches; this tells other bears to keep away. Female bears look after their cubs very carefully and will attack other animals or humans who get too close to them. Cubs are born just before the winter when the bears settle down in a den for three to five months to sleep through the coldest weather. They wake up in the spring when there is plenty of food to eat.

Elephants

The elephant is the largest living land animal; African male elephants are over 3 metres tall and weigh 5 tonnes. An elephant's tooth weighs as much as 4 bags of sugar! Strangely though, the elephant's closest living relative is the hyrax, an animal no bigger than a rabbit.

Elephants are found in the wild only in Africa or Asia. African elephants are the largest; Asian elephants are only 2.5 m tall and have much smaller ears. Female Asian elephants either have very small tusks or none at all. All elephants use their trunks to breathe, smell and suck up water. They can also use them to grab food such as grass, fruit and leaves, or to spray water over themselves to cool down.

Several elephant families live together in a herd. Each family is led by the mother and each herd is led by the strongest male and female. There can only be one dominant male so, as young males become adults, they have to leave. They may fight other males to join a new herd, or they may live alone.

Elephants are social creatures and look after each other in an amazing way. When a baby is about to be born the herd surrounds the mother to protect her, while another female helps her in the birth. The herd will look after an injured elephant and even in death the group shows concern – often covering the dead body with leaves and staying with it for days.

Gorillas

Gorillas belong to the same group of animals as humans. Gorillas and humans are similar, not just in the way they look, but also in the way they behave.

Gorillas live in family groups, led by a large male called a silverback. Each silverback has several females in his family. Mothers have one baby at a time and will not have the next one until the first is five years old. Babies cling tightly to their mother for the first year but, as they get older, they get braver.

Young males leave the group when they are 12 years old. They go in search of females so that they can start their own family groups. Males prefer not to fight; instead they stand tall and thump their chests to scare their rivals away.

Gorillas are vegetarians and feed mainly on leaves and fruit. They live in dense forests where they can spend most of the day collecting food. Gorillas do not often climb trees, except to sleep in. They build nests from plant stems woven in to the branches of trees.

There are three types of gorilla; the western lowland gorilla,

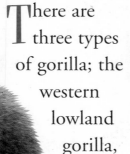

the eastern lowland gorilla and the mountain gorilla. All wild gorillas live in Africa, but sadly there are not many of them left. Gorillas have suffered at the hands of hunters for many years and their forest homes are being cut down. There may be only 450 mountain gorillas left in the wild and conservationists are very worried about their chances of survival. The lowland gorillas are not quite so close to extinction – yet.

Bats

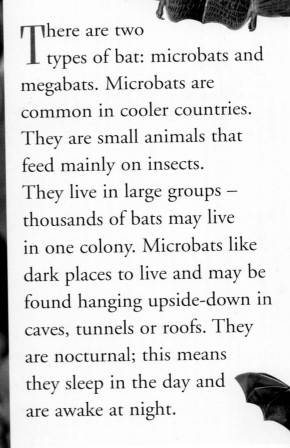

Bats may be very good at flying but they are mammals, not birds. This means they have fur, give birth to their young and feed them with milk. Bats are found in most parts of the world, except the Arctic Circle.

There are two types of bat: microbats and megabats. Microbats are common in cooler countries. They are small animals that feed mainly on insects. They live in large groups – thousands of bats may live in one colony. Microbats like dark places to live and may be found hanging upside-down in caves, tunnels or roofs. They are nocturnal; this means they sleep in the day and are awake at night.

Microbats are hunters and use their sense of smell and hearing to find prey at night. They also use a sense called 'echolocation' to find food; they send out a sound which hits objects around them and then echoes back to their ears, telling the bats the size and position of those objects.

The largest megabat has a wingspan of 1.7 m. These bats live in warmer climates and are often fruit-eaters. They usually feed during the day and have large eyes to help them find food.

The most famous bat of all is the vampire bat. Found in North and Central America, the vampire bat feeds on blood taken from cows, horses, pigs and sometimes humans. Taking the blood does little harm to the animals, but vampires often spread a disease called rabies which can wipe out whole herds of cattle.

Zebras

In the dry, hot grasslands of Africa herds of zebras stand and graze, keeping their ears pricked and their eyes peeled for any lurking lions. Like other wild horses zebras stay in a group for safety.

Zebras are one of many types of African grazing animals that are hunted by lions and hyenas. Their black and white stripes seem to make them easy targets, but actually the stripes confuse the animals that hunt them. When standing together the outline of each animal becomes blurred, and the predator may just see a large pattern of stripes and not be able to pick out one zebra to chase.

A baby zebra is called a foal and it can stand almost as soon as it is born. Young grazing animals have to be strong to be able to survive and zebra foals can keep up with their mothers when they are only a few hours old. A foal recognises its mother by her smell. Zebras may all look alike to us, but they each have different patterns of stripes and the zebras know each other by looking at their stripes and by their smell.

There are many zebras both in the wild and in zoos around the world. A hundred years ago a different type of zebra lived, called quaggas. They had stripes only on the front half of their bodies, the back half was brown. All the quaggas were killed by farmers in South Africa who feared that their crops would be eaten by them.

Lions

Lions, like tigers, cheetahs and leopards, belong to the great cat family. They are meat-eaters and use sharp, hooked claws and powerful jaws to catch their prey.

Years ago, lions lived wild in Asia and Africa. Because people have moved in to their living areas they are now found in the wild only in Africa where they live on the huge grasslands. Lions mainly hunt large grazing animals, such as antelope and zebra.

Unlike the other great cats, lions prefer to live in family groups called prides. The females in a pride are usually related to one another and stay together for life. Baby lions are called cubs and there are between one and four cubs in a litter.

The males join a pride to mate but usually only stay for a few years before younger, stronger males fight them off to take over the pride themselves. The older males then roam the grasslands alone, unless they can take over another pride.

Lions spend nearly all day asleep or resting in the hot African sun. They hunt in the evenings when the air is cooler. The females are the best hunters; once they have chosen their victim, such as an antelope, they all surround it, hidden by the long grass. With a spurt of energy they chase the prey, reaching speeds of 50 kph. A leap onto the antelope's back, and a swift bite into its neck is enough to kill it. The meal is then shared with the whole pride.

The Future

Wild animals are important; we need to protect them. The best way to do this is to make sure they can stay living in the wild. Unfortunately many animals' homes are lost every day as people cut down forests and jungles to plant crops. Living in the wild is difficult for some animals because they are hunted, not for food, but for their skin, their oils or ivory.

Some countries keep their wildlife in National Parks. Here they are protected from hunters and visitors can come to watch them. These are good places to learn about wild animals. The first National Park was set up in Yellowstone, in the USA, in 1872. It is home to many animals, such as grizzly bears and buffalo. In India, National Parks were set up to save the tiger, which came very close to becoming extinct.

Many countries have zoos where they keep wild animals from around the world. The best zoos try to give the animals fields or cages that are like their homes in the wild, with lots of space and plenty to do. These zoos often have breeding programmes; they help their animals to have young. This means no more animals need to be taken from the wild to fill the zoos.

A zoo success story is that of the Arabian oryx, a type of antelope. It had become extinct in the wild, although some were still alive in zoos. These were collected from all round the world and set free in their natural desert home where they formed a new herd.

Further Information

Places to Visit

Flamingo Theme Park and Zoo, The Rectory, Kirby Misperton, Malton, North Yorkshire, YO17 6UX. Telephone: 01653 668287.

Glasgow Zoopark, Caulder Park, Uddingston, Glasgow, G71 7RZ. Telephone: 0141 771 1185.

Highland Wildlife Park, Kincraig, Kingussie, Invernesshire, PH21 1NL. Telephone: 01540 651270.

Howletts Wild Animal Park, Bekesbourne, near Canterbury, Kent, CT4 5EL. Telephone: 01227 721410.

Jersey Zoo, Jersey Wildlife Preservation Trust, Les Augres Manor, Trinity, Jersey, JE3 5BP. Telephone: 01534 864666.

Knowlsey Safari Park, Prescot, Merseyside, L34 4AN. Telephone: 0151 430 9009.

London Zoo, Regent's Park, London, NW1 4RY. Telephone: 0171 722 3333.

Longleat Safari Park, Longleat, Warminster, Wiltshire, BA12 7NW. Telephone: 01985 844400.

Manor House Wildlife Park, St Florence, Tenby, Pembrokeshire, SA70 8RJ. Telephone: 01646 651201.

Monkey Sanctuary, Looe, Cornwall, PL13 1NZ. Telephone: 01503 262532.

Natural History Museum, Cromwell Road, London, SW7 5BD. Telephone: 0171 938 9123.

Welsh Mountain Zoo, The Old Highway, Colwyn Bay, LL28 5UY. Telephone: 01492 532938.

Whipsnade Wild Animal Park, Dunstable, Bedfordshire, LU6 2LF. Telephone: 0990 200 123.

Further Reading

Animal Reproduction by David Burnie, Dorling Kindersley.
Amazing Nature by Michael Chinery, Kingfisher.
Ecology by Richard Spurgeon, Usborne.
Gorilla by Ian Redmond, Dorling Kindersley.
Grassland Wildlife by Kamini Khanduri, Usborne.
Mountain Wildlife by Anna Clayboune & Antonia Cunningham, Usborne.
Nature at Risk by Rosie Harlow & Sally Morgan, Kingfisher.
Rainforest Animals by Michael Chinery, Kingfisher.

Picture Credits

All pictures courtesy of **Still Pictures: Kevin Schafer** 8; **Thomas D. Mangelsen** 10-11; **Klein/Hubert** 12; **Gerald Lacz** 13; **Alain Compost** 14; **Schafer & Hill** 15; **Klein/Hubert** 16; **Dave Watts** 17; **Kevin Schafer** 19; **Patryck Vaucoulon** 20; **Fred Bruemmer** 21; **J & A Visage** 22; **Carl R. Sams II** 23; **Jany Sauvenet** 24; **Michel Gunther** 25; **Peter Weimann** 26; **Peter Weimann** 27; **Yves Lefevre** 28; **M. & C. Denis-Huot** 29; **Steve Kaufman** 30-31; **Mark Carwardine** 31; **M. & C. Denis-Huot** 32; **Mathieu Laboureur** 33; **Kevin Schafer** 34-35; **Jose Kalpers** 35; **Roland Seitre** 36; **B. Odeur** 36-37; **Nigel J. Dennis** 38-39; **M. & C. Denis-Huot** 39; **Fritz Polking** 40; **Nicolas Granier** 41; **M. & C. Denis-Huot** 42; **Michel Gunther** 43.